C0-BIY-899

520
COU

Couper, Heather

C.1

Astronomy

DATE			

MURRAY WRIGHT
HIGH SCHOOL LIBRARY

© THE BAKER & TAYLOR CO.

Art Director	Charles Matheson
Art Editor	Ben White
Editor	Peter Marriott
Illustrators	Denis Bishop
	Chris Forsey
	Hayward Art Group
	Jim Robins

© Aladdin Books Ltd

Designed and produced by
Aladdin Books Ltd
70 Old Compton Street
London W1

First published in the
United States in 1983 by
Franklin Watts
387 Park Avenue South
New York, NY 10016

ISBN 531-04651-6

Library of Congress
Catalog Card No: 83-50112

Printed in Belgium

All rights reserved

Franklin Watts Science World

Astronomy

Heather Couper and Nigel Henbest

Series Editor: Lionel Bender

MURRAY WRIGHT
HIGH SCHOOL LIBRARY

FRANKLIN WATTS
New York · London · Toronto · Sydney

Introduction

Astronomy is the study of all the matter and all the space in the Universe. The Universe is so incredibly vast that we can only just begin to understand the distances between the stars and planets. In fact we have had to invent a new measure for these distances – the light year. A light year is the distance that light, which has a speed of about 300,000 km/sec (186,000 miles/sec), travels in a year – it works out to be over 60,000 times the distance of the Earth to the Sun!

Our Sun is only a tiny fraction of a light year away from us, while the next nearest star to us is 4.3 light years away. Our galaxy (a large island group of stars; including our own) is about 100,000 light years in diameter, and other galaxies are many billions of light years away.

The light that takes so long to reach us from these huge distances shows us these objects as they were when the light left them and not as they are now, so we can see into the distant past and learn much about the history of the Universe and how it began. And by studying the light and other radiation given off by stars and galaxies, astronomers can begin to understand how they generate their huge quantities of energy.

Although astronomy has been studied since the earliest times it is only in relatively recent times that the sophisticated equipment necessary to study the Universe in detail has been developed. There is much more yet to be learned. This book introduces this exciting science and shows many of the objects such as planets and meteors that you can observe for yourself.

Earth is one of nine planets traveling around our local star, the Sun, to form the Solar System. In its turn, the Sun is a member of a vast spiral system of 100 billion stars we call our Milky Way Galaxy – or simply, the Galaxy. The Galaxy belongs to a small cluster of about 50 galaxies called the Local Group. The Universe is made up of clusters and "superclusters" of galaxies separated from each other by vast distances of nearly empty space. There are estimated to be a staggering 10 thousand billion billion stars in the Universe as we know it.

The Solar System

Our Galaxy

Contents

Local galaxies

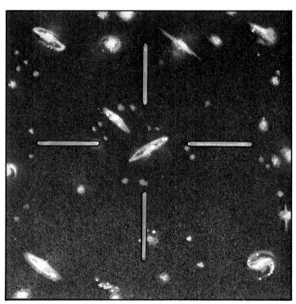

The Universe

Looking into Space

With the naked eye, we can only see a few of the millions upon millions of different objects in the Universe. We can see the Moon (which goes around the Earth) and five of the other planets circling the Sun, because they reflect the Sun's light. In the background we can see a few thousand stars in a dark night sky.

But there are many objects in the sky that are too faint for us to see, for example the three outermost planets – Uranus, Neptune and Pluto. And our unaided eyes cannot see the millions of fainter and very distant stars – or the even more remote galaxies.

To study these faint objects, astronomers use optical telescopes. An optical telescope collects light with a large lens, like a magnifying glass, or a huge curved mirror, similar to a shaving mirror. The lens or mirror is so large that it collects a great amount of light, and can enable us to see these almost invisible bodies.

But even the largest optical telescopes cannot show us everything in the Universe. Some objects are completely dark. But they often produce electromagnetic radiation of wavelengths that are different from that of "visible" light. Tiny dark stars called neutron stars are natural broadcasters of radio waves, so a very sensitive radio set – a "radio telescope" – can pick them up. Astronomers now use many different types of "telescopes" to pick up the different kinds of electromagnetic radiation that we receive from space. The study of these radiations has led astronomers to unravel some of the secrets of the Universe.

▷ The world's second-largest telescope is housed within this dome-shaped building on top of Palomar Mountain in California. It has a curved mirror 5 m (200 inches) in diameter. The dome protects the telescope from wind, rain and the heat of the Sun. The telescope "looks" through the slit in the giant dome.

More than just light

"Electromagnetic radiation" consists of waves of electricity and magnetism. Different kinds of radiation have different wavelengths. The longest waves are used for radio communication and radar location, microwaves for cooking, and infrared for heating. Next comes light. Ultraviolet tans us, X rays can show our bones, and gamma rays are used to sterilize surgical instruments.

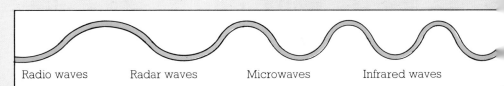

| Radio waves | Radar waves | Microwaves | Infrared waves |

Radio

Radar

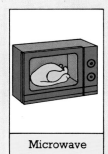

Microwave

Infrared

Visible light   Ultraviolet light   X rays   Gamma rays

Visible light   Ultraviolet   X rays   Gamma rays

Information from Space

Radio Waves

Most radio waves can penetrate down to radio telescopes on the ground, but the longest radio waves are reflected by the highest layer of the atmosphere.

Infrared

Carbon dioxide and water vapor in the atmosphere absorb most infrared. So infrared telescopes are also carried by airplanes, balloons or rockets.

Visible light

Ordinary "visible" light travels down easily through a clear sky. But clouds and air currents near the ground can disturb viewing. So telescopes are built on mountains above the clouds.

Ultraviolet

Most ultraviolet radiation is blocked by a layer of ozone gas in the atmosphere about 50 km (31 miles) up. Ultraviolet telescopes are carried above this layer on rockets or satellites.

X rays

We think of X rays as a "penetrating" radiation which can pass through our flesh. But X rays are easily blocked by the atmosphere. They are studied from satellites or rockets.

Gamma rays

The shortest waves of all, gamma rays, are blocked by the atmosphere too. But some penetrate down to a height where they can be studied from high-flying balloons.

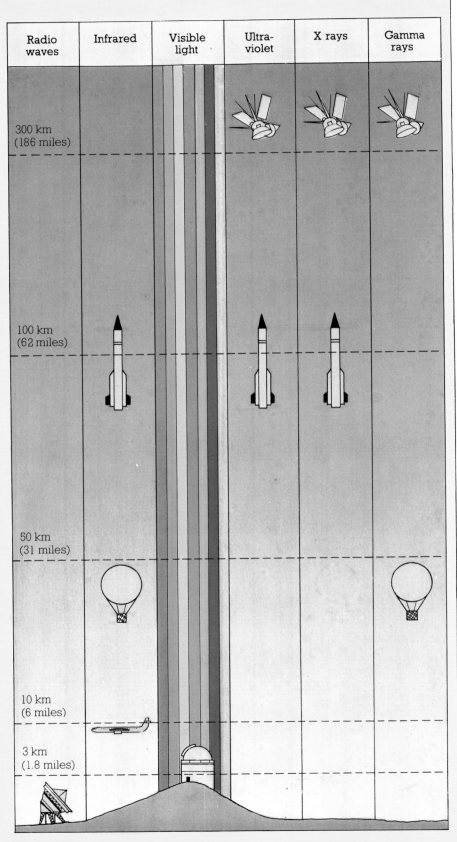

Collecting Information

A radio telescope has a reflecting "dish" to direct radio waves onto a sensitive radio receiver directly above it. It can work in all weathers, night and day. An astronomer uses an optical telescope as a giant camera to take either ordinary photographs or TV pictures for computer analysis.

A land-based infrared telescope looks similar, but the electronic device which records the radiation must be cooled down to −270°C (−454°F). Telescopes in a satellite convert their information into coded radio signals which are sent back to Earth for analysis.

Radio telescope

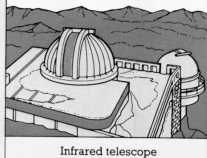

Infrared telescope

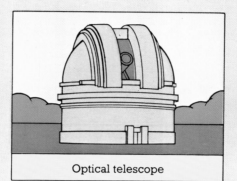

Optical telescope

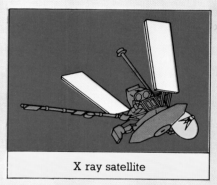

X ray satellite

Looking for Yourself

Observing stars

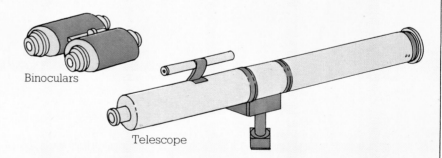

Binoculars

Telescope

Without any kind of telescope, you can spot the closest planets, and every night a few meteors, or "shooting stars", will also be visible. Binoculars will show a lot more; stars too faint for the naked eye; and the fuzzy patches which are distant galaxies, or nebulae where new stars are made. You can also see the largest craters on the Moon and Jupiter's four main satellites. A small telescope reveals hundreds of craters on the Moon, the changing appearance of Venus as it circles the Sun, and the glorious rings of Saturn.

The Sun

Without the Sun, we would not be here to observe the Universe. The Sun is our local star, and we depend on it totally. The Earth is just one of its family of nine planets. The Sun is a gigantic, spinning ball of hot gases, pouring out radiation into space. It gives just the right amount of light and heat to let us live comfortably. Over millions of years it has provided energy which, among other things, has made possible the formation of oil and coal, two of the most important fuels we use today. If we could duplicate the way in which the Sun produces its energy, we would have an almost unlimited supply of cheap and safe power.

The Sun affects the Earth in other ways, many of which we are just starting to learn about. Long-term climate changes, like the Ice Ages, for example, and even our daily weather patterns, may have their origins in the Sun. The Sun is also a stormy body, and its storms can sometimes affect us on Earth. They may cause radio blackouts – the loss of radio communication. However, we are lucky that the Sun is relatively constant as stars go. Many other stars vary in their output of light and heat, and if the Sun were a variable star, life on Earth would be impossible.

As yet, there is no direct evidence that other stars have planets like the Sun. But the Sun is such a typical star that it is difficult to believe it could be unique.

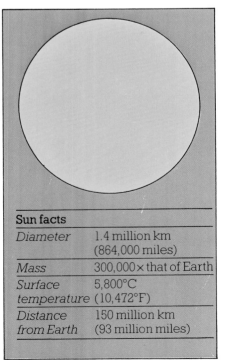

Sun facts	
Diameter	1.4 million km (864,000 miles)
Mass	300,000 × that of Earth
Surface temperature	5,800°C (10,472°F)
Distance from Earth	150 million km (93 million miles)

Visible light

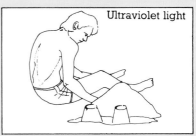

Ultraviolet light

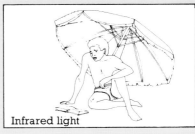

Infrared light

The Sun's radiation
The Sun's radiation allows us to see things by visible light, while ultraviolet light can give us a tan, and infrared gives the Earth its warmth.

◁ It is only too easy to have too much of the Sun's energy even though it has traveled to us across 150 million km (93 million miles) of space. Fortunately, much of the harmful radiation – X rays for example – is absorbed by our atmosphere.

The Sun's Energy

WARNING
NEVER LOOK DIRECTLY AT THE SUN, EVEN THROUGH DARK GLASSES. IT WILL DAMAGE YOUR SIGHT!

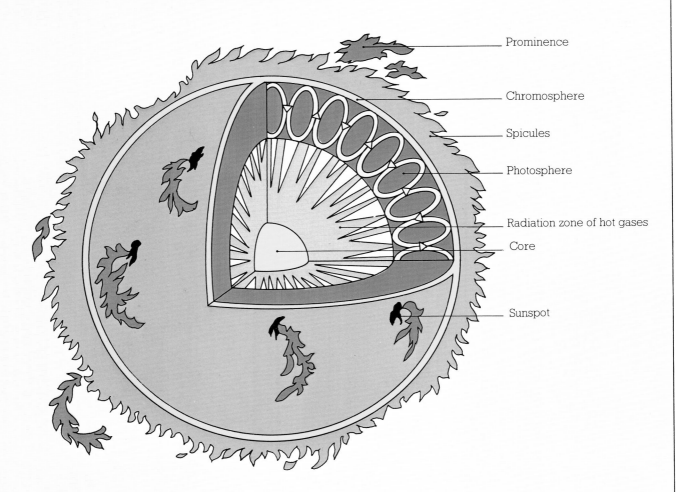

- Prominence
- Chromosphere
- Spicules
- Photosphere
- Radiation zone of hot gases
- Core
- Sunspot

The Sun's energy

The Sun is over 330,000 times more massive than the Earth, and its matter is subjected to a very strong gravitational pull. Thus, it is very hot and compressed. Its core is very hot, close to 14 million °C (25 million °F). Solids and liquids cannot exist at these temperatures, therefore, the Sun is made up of gas, mostly hydrogen, at intense pressure. Under these extreme conditions the nuclei of four hydrogen atoms are fused together to form the nucleus of a helium atom. The mass of a helium

The fusion reaction

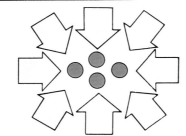

Hydrogen atoms squeezed under great pressure of gravity

A Helium atom is formed and energy is released

nucleus is slightly less than that of four hydrogen nuclei and, this lost mass is released as energy. This reaction keeps our star shining for billions of years. Every second, the Sun converts millions of tons of itself into energy. The fiery visible surface of the Sun is called the photosphere. Above it, in the chromosphere, long jets of hot gas (spicules) give the Sun a slightly hairy appearance. Beyond this is the corona which forms a halo around the Sun.

Sunspots

In places, the Sun's surface is interrupted by spots which are dark because they are more than 1,000°C (1,832°F) cooler than the photosphere. Sunspots sometimes cover millions of square kilometers. Roughly every eleven years, spots, prominences and flares (solar storms) build up to a maximum activity as the strength of the Sun's surface magnetic field ebbs and flows. Sunspots can be viewed safely with a telescope by projecting the Sun's image onto a sheet of white paper.

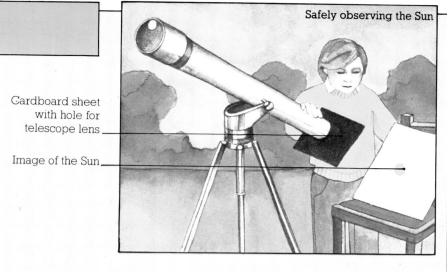

Safely observing the Sun

Cardboard sheet with hole for telescope lens

Image of the Sun

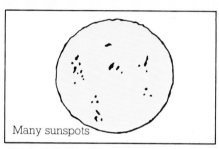

Many sunspots

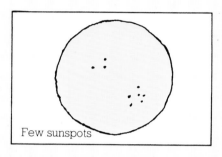

Few sunspots

The Solar Wind

The Sun pours out a stream of electrically charged particles, called the solar wind. This reaches gale-force during a solar maximum. After the most violent flares, the wind crashes into the Earth's magnetosphere – the outermost magnetic layer of its atmosphere, beyond the Van Allen belts of charged particles. Most of the wind is deflected off into space, but some travels down the Earth's magnetic field to our North and South Poles, creating the spectacular northern and southern lights.

The northern lights

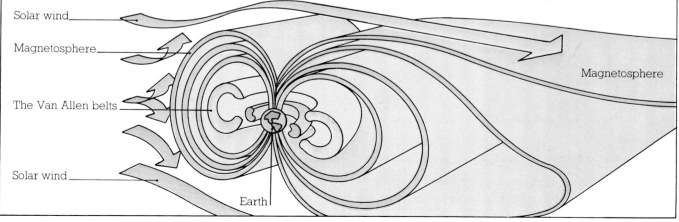

Solar wind

Magnetosphere

The Van Allen belts

Solar wind

Earth

Magnetosphere

The Earth and the Moon

We live on the planet Earth, a ball of rock 12,750 km (7,923 miles) in diameter. Like all the planets, the Earth spins, or rotates, on its axis and orbits the Sun. It completes an orbit in one year, traveling through space at a speed of about 100,000 km/h (62,000 miles/h).

But the Earth is not alone. It has a companion on its travels – the Moon – which orbits the Earth once a month. The Moon is quite a substantial world, one-quarter the size of the Earth, and many astronomers think of the Earth and Moon as a "double planet."

But the two worlds are very different. The Moon is a dead planet. It has no volcanoes or geological activity, it is airless, waterless and lifeless. Without an atmosphere to protect it, the Moon's surface is heated to 105°C (221°F) during its daytime, and cools to −155°C (−247°F) at night.

The Earth is active, lush and fertile. It has spectacular active volcanoes. Its surface is cloaked by an atmosphere which we can breathe, and which also keeps the temperature quite constant. Two-thirds of the Earth is covered by oceans of water, and most of the land area has vegetation covering the rocks and soil. Our planet supports millions of different living things – plants, insects, birds, mammals and humans.

▷ From their orbit above the Moon, the Apollo astronauts saw the distant Earth as a beautiful blue planet.
Because the Moon orbits the Earth in the same time as it revolves, it always keeps the same "face" toward the Earth.

Earth facts	
Diameter	12,750 km (7,923 miles)
Rotation period	23 hours 56 minutes
Orbit around the Sun	365.25 days
Average surface temperature.	15°C (59°F)
Distance from Sun	150 million km (93 million miles)

Moon facts	
Diameter	3,476 km (2,160 miles)
Rotation period	27.3 days
Orbit around Earth	27.3 days
Mass	0.012 that of Earth
Gravity	0.17 that of Earth
Surface temperature	Day: 105°C (221°F) Night: −155°C (−247°F)
Distance from Earth	384,400 km (238,620 miles)

The American Apollo astronauts brought back samples of Moon-rocks to reveal the story of the dead Moon. Geologists studying the rocks have found that the Moon, like all the planets, formed from smaller rocky worlds which collided. The last of these rocks to fall hit the Moon with such force that they blasted out huge round holes with high rims – the Moon's craters. The biggest craters are thousands of kilometers wide, and their rims make mountain chains as high as Mount Everest. Later, the Moon's surface oozed out streams of molten lava. This filled the largest craters and solidified to make dark lava plains. But these lava flows ceased almost 4,000 million years ago, and the Moon's atmosphere leaked away into space because its gravity was too weak to hold onto it.

Because Earth is a more massive body, it has a strong enough gravitational pull to hold onto its atmosphere. And atmospheric pressure means that its water has not been lost to space. The water in rainfall, rivers, and glaciers has worn away the Earth's original cratered surface – that which it had before it cooled down and developed an atmosphere capable of resisting all but the largest intruders from space.

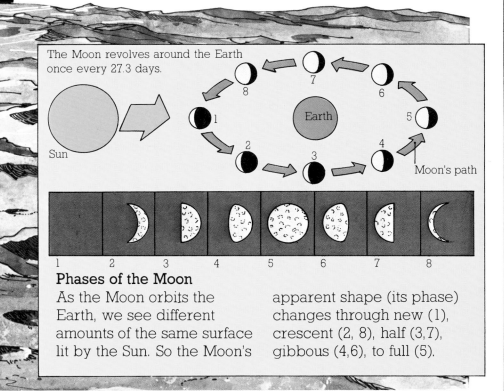

The Moon revolves around the Earth once every 27.3 days.

Sun

Earth

Moon's path

Phases of the Moon

As the Moon orbits the Earth, we see different amounts of the same surface lit by the Sun. So the Moon's apparent shape (its phase) changes through new (1), crescent (2, 8), half (3,7), gibbous (4,6), to full (5).

Day and Night

Observing the rotation of the Earth

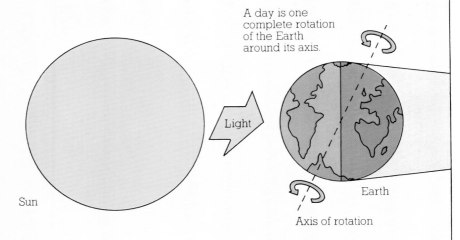

Sun

A day is one complete rotation of the Earth around its axis.

Light

Earth

Axis of rotation

The Sun only shines on one side of the Earth at a time. As the Earth spins around, each part of the Earth's surface in turn receives the light of day and the dark of night.

The Earth turns in a counter-clockwise direction – if you look at it from above the North Pole. As the Earth rotates the Sun apparently rises in the Eastern sky. The Sun's apparent motion from

East to West every day can be shown by observing the motion of a shadow cast by a stick placed vertically in the ground. Eventually the Sun "sets" in the West and night falls.

Seasons

As the Sun's light and heat falls on the Earth, it is more spread out near the poles because it covers a larger area of ground. So the polar regions are cooler than those at the equator. But the Earth's axis is tilted in space. So at any one place, when the Sun is high in the sky and its heat is more concentrated on the ground, it is summer – while six months later, when the planet is at the opposite side of its orbit, the Sun appears low in the sky, its heat is more spread out and it is winter. The Northern hemisphere has its summer in June and the Southern hemisphere in December.

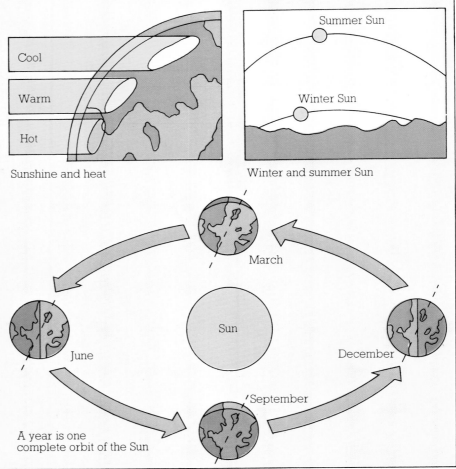

Cool

Warm

Hot

Sunshine and heat

Summer Sun

Winter Sun

Winter and summer Sun

March

Sun

June

December

September

A year is one complete orbit of the Sun

Tides

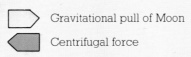

Gravitational pull of Moon

Centrifugal force

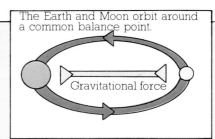

The Earth and Moon orbit around a common balance point.

Gravitational force

Earth

Tide

Tide

Moon

The tide coming in

At the seashore, we can watch the tide coming in and going out twice each day. Tides are caused by two forces – centrifugal force and the pull of the Moon's gravity. The Moon and Earth revolve around a joint balance point. On the side of the Earth furthest from the Moon, this motion creates a centrifugal force which causes the ocean to bulge outward. On the side of the Earth nearest the Moon the Moon's gravity pulls the ocean outward. Because the Earth revolves, each area of ocean will experience both pulls in the course of a day.

Eclipses

WARNING
NEVER LOOK DIRECTLY AT THE SUN, EVEN THROUGH DARK GLASSES. IT WILL DAMAGE YOUR SIGHT!

As the Earth and Moon orbit one another, the shadow of one can fall on the other. When the Moon moves into the Earth's shadow the Moon almost fades from sight. This is a lunar eclipse. Much more spectacular is a solar eclipse, when the Moon lies between the Sun and Earth. If we are in the exact region of the Moon's smaller shadow, we see the Sun's glowing disk being blocked off by the dark New Moon. As the Sun is hidden, everything suddenly goes dark. It is a rare chance to study the Sun's beautiful outer atmosphere, which is usually lost in the brilliance of the Sun.

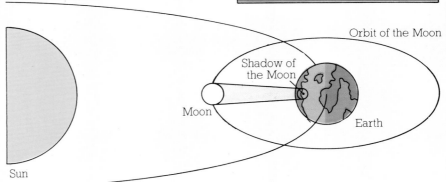

Orbit of the Earth

Orbit of the Moon

Shadow of the Moon

Moon

Earth

Sun

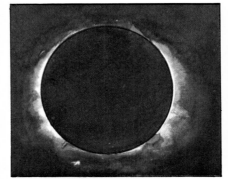

A total eclipse: the Moon covers the Sun completely, and the Sun's atmosphere can be seen.

A partial eclipse: the Moon only passes over part of the Sun

The Solar System

The Solar System is the family of objects which orbit the Sun. The most important are the nine planets. These range in size from the gas giant Jupiter, eleven times the Earth's diameter, down to tiny Pluto, one-quarter the size of our planet. Mercury is the closest-in of the planets, at a distance of 57.9 million km (35.9 million miles) from the Sun, while far-flung Pluto orbits so far out that the Sun looks merely like a very bright star 5,941 million km (3,692 million miles) away.

The Solar System also includes many smaller bodies. Most planets have satellites or moons of their own, ranging in size from worlds as big as Mercury (such as Jupiter's moon Ganymede) to the tiny chunks of rock and ice that make up the rings of Saturn. Hundreds of thousands of "minor planets" or asteroids follow orbits between Mars and Jupiter, and comets dive in from beyond Pluto's orbit to graze the Sun.

In addition the space between bodies is not completely empty. Comets leave behind tiny grains of dust – the size of sand grains and smaller – between the inner planets of the Solar System. And a "wind" of hot gases and magnetic fields is continuously blowing outward from the Sun's surface, past the Earth and into the deep space far beyond Pluto.

▽ There are nine known planets – though some astronomers would now call Pluto a large asteroid. The four inner rocky planets are quite small. The four giant outer planets are made largely of gases.

		Number of moons
1	Mercury	0
2	Venus	0
3	Earth	1
4	Mars	2
5	Jupiter	16
6	Saturn	23
7	Uranus	5
8	Neptune	2
9	Pluto	1

The Sun

The planets of the Solar System

All the planets travel in orbits around the Sun, moving in the same direction (counter-clockwise if you look from above the Sun's North Pole). Most of the nearly circular orbits lie in the same plane, except for the slightly tilted and elongated orbits of Mercury and Pluto. Pluto's orbit is so elongated that at times it comes closer to the Sun than Neptune. The length of time that a planet takes to orbit the Sun (its year) depends on its distance from the Sun. It varies from only 88 Earth days for Mercury through 1 year for Earth, to about 250 Earth years for Pluto.

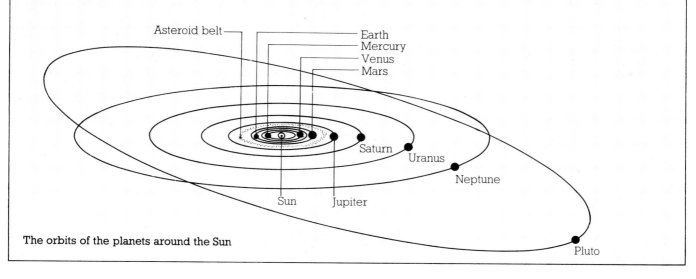

Asteroid belt — Earth — Mercury — Venus — Mars — Saturn — Uranus — Neptune — Sun — Jupiter — Pluto

The orbits of the planets around the Sun

6 7 8 9

The Origin of the Solar System

The Sun and the Solar System were born 4.6 billion years ago as a huge cloud of gas and dust began to contract under gravity. A nearby supernova (an exploding star) may have given it the first "kick" to make it collapse. The contracting cloud spun faster and faster, gradually becoming disk-shaped. At the center the young Sun started to form, while in the cooler disk, gas and dust grains collided to make the beginnings of the planets and their moons. Since a final violent episode about 3.8 billion years ago, when nearly all the stray pieces of matter were mopped up by the planets, the Solar System has hardly changed.

Collapsing gas cloud

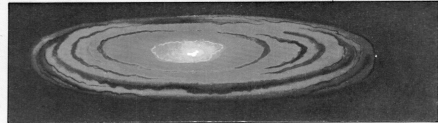

The Sun and planets start to form

The planets and satellites form

Temperature and Life

Life on Earth

Mars · Mercury

Too hot

Life zone

Too cold

Earth

Venus

Sun

Every star has a zone around it called the "ecosphere" (sphere of life) where the temperature would be right for life as we know it to exist. In our Solar System, Earth sits in the middle of this zone. Venus is just inside it, where the temperature is too high, while Mars lies outside, where it is too cold. As yet, we do not know for certain if any other stars have planets – let alone planets situated inside habitable zones.

Gravity

Gravity

The Atmosphere

The Earth and the Moon

Gravity is the force of attraction that every object feels for another. The more massive an object, the stronger is its pull, and the pull is greater the closer together the two objects are. Your own body's gravity attracts the Earth; but the Earth is so much more massive that it holds you down to its surface. When you throw a ball in the air, the Earth's gravity pulls it downward, and in just the same way, Earth's gravity holds down its relatively thick atmosphere. At a longer range, the Moon's pull of gravity raises tides in the oceans. And the Sun's gravity keeps the planets around it. They don't fall directly into the Sun, however, because the centrifugal force created by the speed of their motion in orbit around the Sun exactly balances the pull of the Sun's gravity.

Planetary Movement

Because the Sun's pull of gravity on the Earth is greater than that felt by more distant Mars, the Earth has to experience a greater centrifugal force. It creates this by traveling faster in its orbit. This means that it periodically overtakes Mars. Thus, as seen from Earth, when Earth overtakes Mars (A-E in the picture) Mars appears to slow down and do a loop in the sky. For a short while (from B-C) it actually seems to move backward.

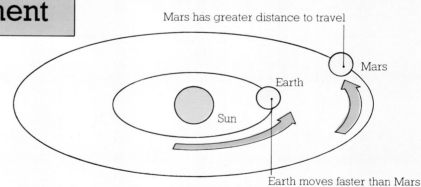

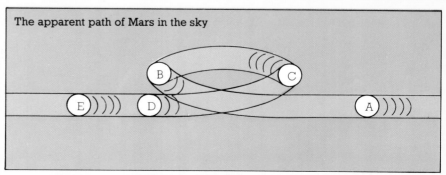

The apparent path of Mars in the sky

Mercury

Mars

The Planets

Mercury
The surface of tiny airless Mercury shows signs of heavy bombardment from space. Its day temperature of 350°C (662°F) falls to −170°C (−274°F) at night.

Venus
The surface temperature of Venus is 465°C (869°F) and it has an atmosphere of carbon dioxide with sulfuric acid clouds. Below the clouds are high mountains and volcanic plateaux.

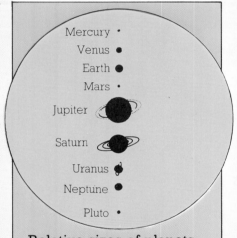

Mercury ·
Venus •
Earth ●
Mars ·
Jupiter ●
Saturn ●
Uranus ●
Neptune ●
Pluto ·

Relative sizes of planets
Compared to the Sun, all planets are small – even the four huge gas giants. Pluto is smallest of all.

Mars
The red soil of Mars can be whipped up into tremendous duststorms by winds in the thin atmosphere. Occasional clouds contain ice, but the surface is too cold to support life as we know it.

Jupiter
So big that it could swallow 1,300 Earths, Jupiter has a deep atmosphere of ammonia, methane and hydrogen, covering a small core of solid hydrogen. It spins so rapidly that its clouds are drawn out into belts around the planet.

Venus

Jupiter

Saturn

Neptune

Saturn

Astronomers have found 23 moons around Saturn. The largest, Titan, has a dense nitrogen atmosphere. Saturn's famous rings, of which there are several thousand, are made up of chunks of rock and ice.

Uranus

Discovered in 1781, Uranus is another gas giant, surrounded by at least nine thin rings circling its equator. Because it travels around the Sun pole-first, the rings look vertical rather than horizontal, when seen from the Earth.

Planet	Mean distance from Sun	
	millions of km	(millions of miles)
1 Pluto	5941.0 km	(3691.7 miles)
2 Neptune	4496.6 km	(2794.2 miles)
3 Uranus	2869.6 km	(1783.2 miles)
4 Saturn	1427.0 km	(886.7 miles)
5 Jupiter	778.3 km	(483.6 miles)
6 Mars	227.9 km	(141.6 miles)
7 Earth	149.6 km	(92.9 miles)
8 Venus	108.2 km	(67.2 miles)
9 Mercury	57.9 km	(35.9 miles)

Neptune

The fourth gas-giant, Neptune, is similar in size to Uranus. Much of Neptune remains a mystery. It was pinpointed after a special search in 1846 because its gravity was pulling Uranus out of position.

Pluto

Discovered in 1930 as a result of a deliberate search for an object that was disturbing the orbits of Neptune and Uranus, Pluto is too small to have any real effect and it may not be a true planet at all. It has a tiny moon called Charon.

Uranus

Pluto

MURRAY WRIGHT HIGH SCHOOL

3 0552 00106 8380

Satellites

The satellite families of the outer planets are like miniature solar systems, and the individual moons are just as varied as are the planets in the Solar System. The four largest of Jupiter's sixteen known moons are all different. Callisto is the most heavily-cratered body in the Solar System. Ganymede is cratered too, but its surface is also covered in wide bands of parallel cracks. The smooth and featureless Europa must be covered with ice. But Io is hot and molten inside, and covered with active volcanoes.

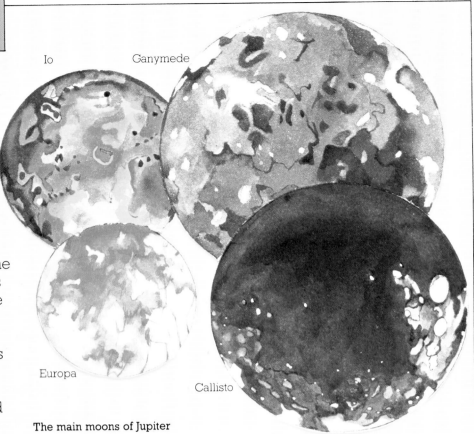

The main moons of Jupiter

Asteroids

Many thousands of pieces of rock and iron ranging from jagged boulders to minor planets 1,000 km (620 miles) across orbit the Sun in a wide belt. These asteroids are probably bits of material that failed to form a planet because of the disruptive pull of Jupiter's gravity. Some asteroids with elongated orbits sometimes pass close to planets. The moons of Mars – Phobos and Deimos – may be captured asteroids, and craters on the Moon may be the result of asteroid collisions.

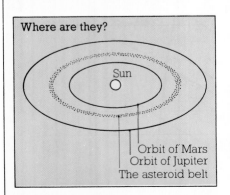

Where are they?

Sun

Orbit of Mars
Orbit of Jupiter
The asteroid belt

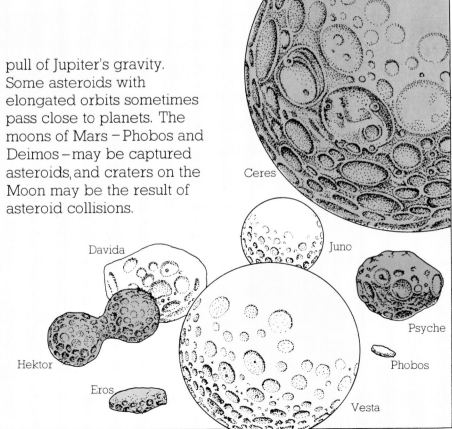

Comets

The nucleus of a comet is a loose ball of frozen gas and rock measuring less than 100 km (62 miles) across. Comets are made of material left over from the birth of the Solar System, and there are millions in a vast cloud surrounding the Solar System beyond the orbit of Pluto. Occasionally, the weak pull of a passing star can send one hurtling in toward the Sun. As the comet races inward, its ices melt and then evaporate, and the nucleus develops a huge shining "coma" of gas around itself. At its closest approach to the Sun, gas and

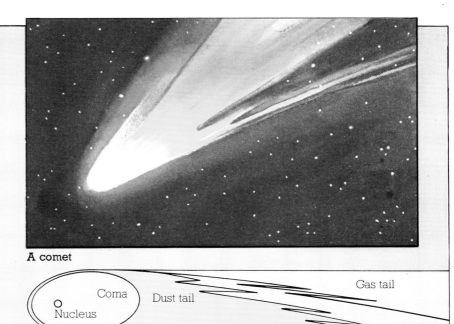

A comet

Nucleus · Coma · Dust tail · Gas tail

dust are forced away as a pair of streaming tails which may be millions of kilometers long. After rounding the Sun, the comet

slowly re-freezes. But it is now trapped within the Solar System, and will continue orbiting the Sun on an elongated path.

Meteors

Eventually all that remains of a comet is fine dust spread along the path of its orbit. During the year, the Earth cuts across a number of comet orbits, and the dust grains plunge into our atmosphere as meteor showers. The meteors are traveling so quickly that they burn up through friction with the air about 100 km (62 miles) up – and we see a brief streak of light (a "shooting star") in the sky. Meteor showers appear to radiate away from a point in the sky. Larger meteors are stray fragments of iron or rock from the asteroid belt.

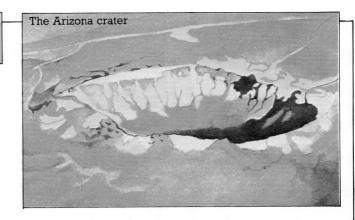

The Arizona crater

When they plunge earthward they look very bright, and sometimes trail sparks of different colors as fragments break off. The largest meteors can survive to land as meteorites. Meteorites weighing more than 100,000 tonnes (98,425 tons) have blasted out huge craters seen in some parts of the Earth.

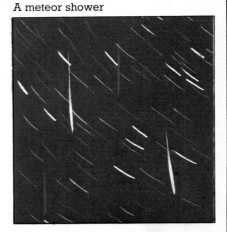

A meteor shower

MURRAY WRIGHT
HIGH SCHOOL LIBRARY

The Starry Skies

On a really clear, dark night, you can see about 3,000 stars. Although they may look like tiny, twinkling dots, this is an illusion. The "twinkling" is caused by the continual shifting of our own atmosphere. Stars are huge balls of luminous gas, many of them far bigger and brighter than our Sun, although they all seem faint because they are so far away. The range in brightness we see among the stars is partly due to differences in size and temperature, and partly due to the fact that they lie at different distances from us.

The ancient astronomers gave names to the brightest stars and made maps of the sky by joining up the stars in imaginary patterns called constellations. These were named after objects or creatures which they resembled.

As the Earth revolves around the Sun, different constellations appear, disappear and reappear at different times of the year. Early civilizations used the apparent motions of the Sun, Moon and stars around the Earth's sky to provide both a daily clock and a yearly calendar. Early sailors and explorers used the stars for navigation: different stars appeared in the sky if they traveled as far north or far south of their starting point. The astronauts on the Apollo 15 lunar mission were able to see many more bright stars against a black background.

▷ Today, star positions are known so precisely that the astronauts on the Apollo 15 lunar mission were able to use them to map the Moon very accurately. Here the Command and Service Module (CSM) orbits the Moon taking simultaneous photographs of the sky and the lunar surface.

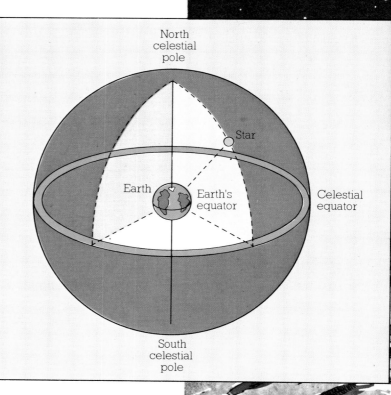

The celestial sphere

On a clear night, the stars appear as if they were painted on a huge dome. Of course, in reality, they are separated by vast tracts of empty space. But we can use a celestial sphere to show the position of the stars as they appear to us in the night sky. The celestial sphere is rather like a globe of the Earth. It has a North and South Pole and an equator that correspond to those of the Earth. Using the sphere, star maps can be created, just as we create maps of the Earth.

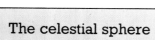

North celestial pole

Star

Earth

Earth's equator

Celestial equator

South celestial pole

Mapping the Moon

Thousands of overlapping sky and Moon photographs were individually cross-referenced. Because the stars' positions are known to such precision, the lunar features could be lined up exactly, so that highly accurate Moon maps could be made.

Stellar photographs

Surface photographs

Mapping the Stars

This star chart shows all the major stars and constellations visible in both the Northern and Southern hemispheres. It is made by "unwrapping" the celestial sphere. This works well for the central part of the chart, but the constellations at the North and South parts of the chart become distorted from their true patterns, so two separate polar charts are made to show these best. A star's position on the chart is given by using latitude and longitude co-ordinates, similar to those used on maps of the Earth. Although the chart shows all the sky, the number of stars that you can actually see depends on your position on the Earth, and on the time of the year. Observers in Europe or the U.S., for example, will never see the Southern Cross, because it lies too far south. And because the Earth rotates around the Sun, the stars appear to wheel from East to West across the sky, and at certain times of the year they disappear in the brightness of our blue daytime sky.

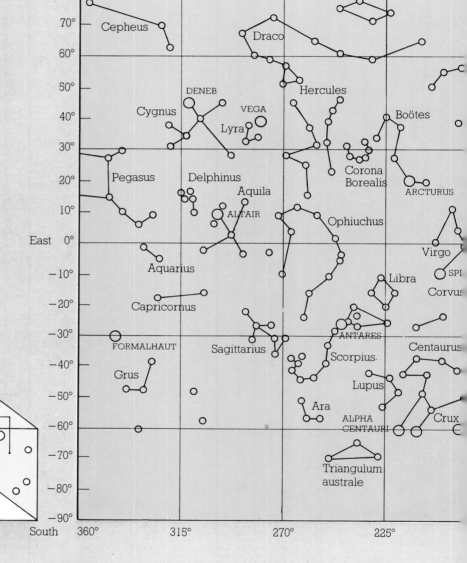

The Celestial Sphere unfolded
Larger stars are the brightest

Stars seen as a constellation
Earth
Stars separated in space

Stars in a constellation

The Constellations

Orion – the Hunter — is one of the most spectacular constellations, and it can be seen from the Northern and Southern hemispheres. It contains the two bright stars, Rigel and Betelgeuse. The brightest star in the sky is nearby Sirius, the Dog star. Ursa Major – the Plough – dominates the northern part of the sky, while the Southern Cross is a striking formation in the Southern hemisphere. Alpha Centauri, in the constellation of Centaurus, is the nearest bright star to our Sun.

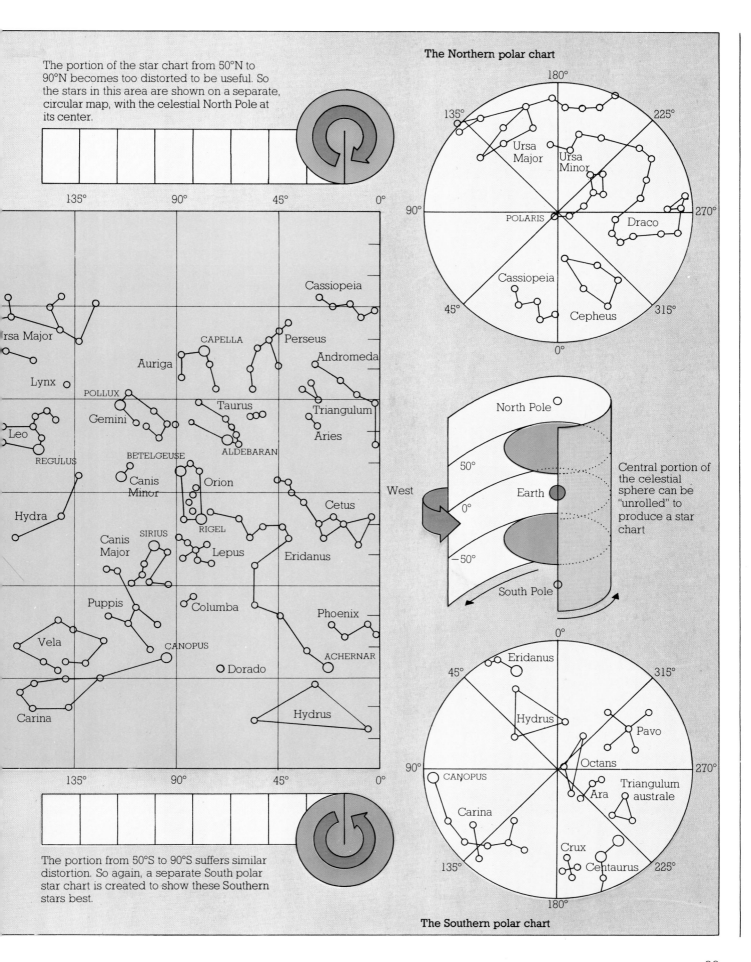

The portion of the star chart from 50°N to 90°N becomes too distorted to be useful. So the stars in this area are shown on a separate, circular map, with the celestial North Pole at its center.

135°   90°   45°   0°

The Northern polar chart

180°

135°

225°

Ursa Major

Ursa Minor

90°

270°

POLARIS

Draco

Cassiopeia

45°

315°

Cepheus

0°

Cassiopeia

Perseus

CAPELLA

Auriga

Andromeda

Ursa Major

POLLUX

Triangulum

Lynx

Taurus

Gemini

Aries

Leo

ALDEBARAN

BETELGEUSE

REGULUS

Canis Minor

Orion

Cetus

Hydra

RIGEL

Canis Major

SIRIUS

Lepus

Eridanus

Puppis

Columba

Phoenix

Vela

CANOPUS

ACHERNAR

Dorado

Carina

Hydrus

North Pole

50°

Central portion of the celestial sphere can be "unrolled" to produce a star chart

West

0°

Earth

–50°

South Pole

0°

Eridanus

45°

315°

Hydrus

Pavo

Octans

90°

270°

CANOPUS

Ara

Triangulum australe

Carina

Crux

135°

225°

Centaurus

180°

135°   90°   45°   0°

The portion from 50°S to 90°S suffers similar distortion. So again, a separate South polar star chart is created to show these Southern stars best.

The Southern polar chart

29

The Lives of Stars

Stars are not unchanging; they are born, will live a long life, but then they will eventually die. Our Sun – an average star – has lived for 5 billion years already and still has about 5 billion years to go. But we can see other stars at different stages of their development, and so we can piece together the story of a star's lifetime.

The raw material of stars is the gas and dust spread extremely thinly throughout our Galaxy. But in places it is clumped into dense, dark clouds. If one of these clouds is given a "squeeze" – either by the effect of nearby masses of dust and gas on the motion of particles within the cloud, or by a star exploding nearby – it will start to collapse. Gravity takes over, and the cloud collapses ever-more quickly, particularly in its central regions. It breaks up into fragments which contract and spin faster and faster as the runaway collapse continues.

The compressed gas suffers a very rapid rise in temperature. At first, we detect this from the infrared (heat) radiation given out by the still-invisible "protostar" fragments inside the cloud. When the central temperature of an individual protostar has reached a few million degrees, the gas suddenly undergoes hydrogen fusion. The resulting energy floods out of the young star, making it shine. This outflow prevents any further collapse, while the surrounding dust shell is blown away. In some cases, billions of dust grains will have stuck together to form an encircling system of planets.

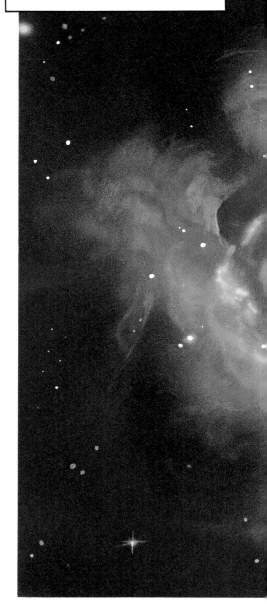

▷ The beautiful Orion Nebula, visible to the unaided eye as a misty patch below the "belt" of the Orion constellation, is just a small part of a vast collapsing gas cloud. It glows brilliantly, excited by fierce ultraviolet radiation from new stars inside.

The energy of a star

The energy produced by fusion in a hydrogen bomb explosion would fuel a star for only the smallest fraction of a second.

The energy generated inside a star's core by the same fusion process begins as powerful penetrating radiation (X rays and gamma rays), and finally escapes into space as less harmful light and heat coming from the star's photosphere.

A hydrogen bomb – fusion

Types of stars

Astronomers classify stars by their color, which is a guide to their surface temperature. The color sequence (from hottest to coolest) runs from O stars (blue-white), B and A stars (white), F and G stars (yellow), K stars (orange) to M stars (red).

Surface temperature	Color
25,000°C 45,000°F Typical star SPICA	Blue-white
10,000°C 18,000°F Typical star SIRIUS	White
6,000°C 10,800°F Typical star SUN	Yellow
4,000°C 7,200°F Typical star ARCTURUS	Orange
3,000°C 5,400°F Typical star BETELGEUSE	Red

A Sun-like Star

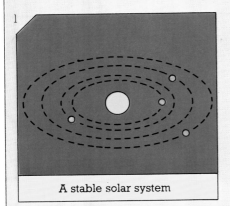

A stable solar system

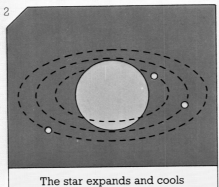

The star expands and cools

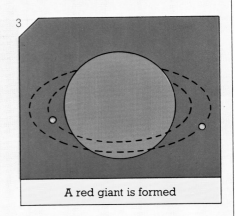

A red giant is formed

A battle against gravity

We can see what is likely to happen to our Sun by looking at similar stars in different stages of their lives. A star can live for billions of years in perfect balance between the outflow of energy from its core, and the inpull of gravity (1). But when all the hydrogen has been converted to helium, the star runs out of fuel. Gravity squeezes the core, heating it up, causing the star's outer layers to billow outward (2). It then settles down temporarily as a huge red giant (3) – perhaps having swallowed a planet or two in the process. Gravity has only a weak hold on the star's outer layers, which gently drift off into space, and we see the core of the old star and its gas shell as a "planetary nebula" (4). As the shell disperses, the core remains as a superdense, collapsed white dwarf star (5) which has no fuel and eventually cools to a dark cinder (6), still circled by its frozen planets.

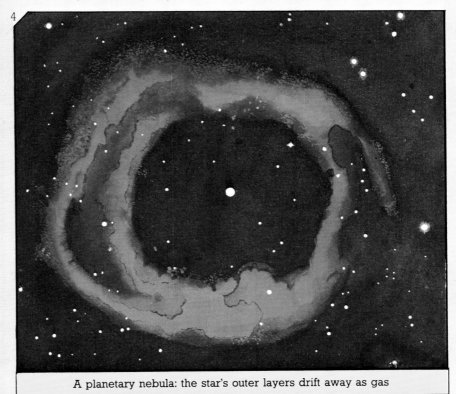

A planetary nebula: the star's outer layers drift away as gas

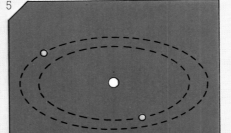

White dwarf and attendant planets

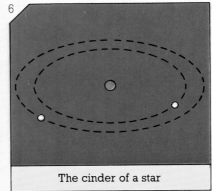

The cinder of a star

A Heavyweight Star

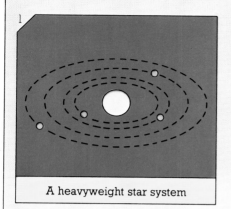

A heavyweight star system

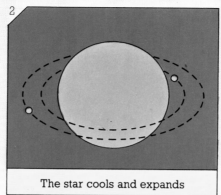

The star cools and expands

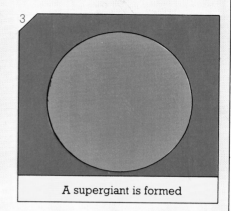

A supergiant is formed

The death of a greedy star

Stars more than five times heavier than the Sun shine very fiercely (1). Sometimes they can use all their hydrogen in less than a million years. The core collapses and the star swells into a supergiant (2,3). Now intense pressure triggers helium fusion in the dense core, and the star has a new source of energy as helium nuclei combine to form carbon. But soon it runs out of helium. Once again, its core collapses and further fusion is triggered. It can go on in this way until it has a core of iron nuclei. However, when it tries to fuse iron, it actually needs to take in energy, and this can only come from a supernova explosion (4). Afterwards, the core may remain as a tiny, super-collapsed neutron star (5) only 15 km (9.3 miles) across. A really heavy star may leave behind a black hole (6), so collapsed that not even light escapes its massive gravitational pull.

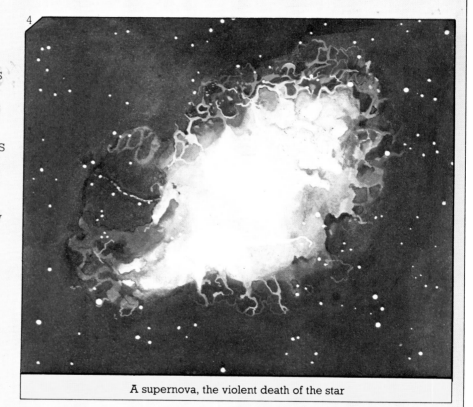

A supernova, the violent death of the star

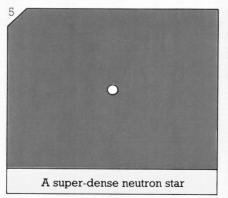

A super-dense neutron star

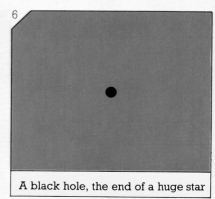

A black hole, the end of a huge star

Our Galaxy

All the stars we see are just a tiny fraction of the 100 billion members of our local star system, the Milky Way Galaxy. The Milky Way is a flat disk-shaped star-island 100,000 light years in diameter. (In contrast, the nearest star to us after the Sun is a mere 4.3 light years away.) Each star in the Galaxy orbits the center – with those nearest the center orbiting fastest. Our Sun takes about 250 million years to complete one orbit.

The Galaxy's central bulge (the nucleus) is made up of relatively old stars, but the surrounding disk is young and active. In the outcurving spiral arms, where the crowding of stars and gas is at its greatest, supernova explosions and gravitational effects trigger star formation – so the arms are studded with glowing nebulae where stars have just been born, and by other hot, relatively short-lived residents – open star clusters and blue supergiant stars. Dark clouds of dust and gas, destined to collapse into stars, line the inner rims of the arms. These block the view of astronomers and so we can only see a small portion of our own Galaxy.

Although most of the stars in the Galaxy are found in the central bulge and spiral arms, there is a huge spherical zone around our Galaxy – the halo – in which many very old stars are spread out thinly. Some of these are concentrated into about 120 globular clusters, each made up of hundreds of thousands of stars. These stars in the globular clusters and halo were the first stars to be created when our Galaxy was born.

▷ This view of our Galaxy shows the yellowish glow from the central nucleus which is made of old, cool stars. In contrast, the gas-rich spiral arms glare with searing radiation from massive, newly formed supergiant stars.

The position of our Sun

Astronomers study the structure of our Galaxy with radio telescopes. The study of radio waves from the cold hydrogen gas between the stars has revealed the Galaxy's spiral structure. Our own position in the Galaxy (shown by a cross, right) is not at all special. We live some 10,000 light years from the center, in or near a spiral arm.

Position of our Sun in the Galaxy

Other Galaxies

Beyond our Galaxy, separated from us by vast tracts of empty space, lie billions of other galaxies. Astronomers have to use powerful telescopes to see them. A few are visible to the unaided eye, like the Andromeda Galaxy. It looks like a twin of the Milky Way, but is nearly half as large again and lies over 2 million light years away. Although many galaxies are spirals or barred spirals, there are a few smaller ones which have not developed spiral arms. The Magellanic Clouds – the nearest galaxies to the Milky Way, visible in the Southern hemisphere, are typical "irregular" galaxies. Elliptical galaxies must have made all their gas into stars very early on. As a result, they are now huge featureless balls of old red stars.

The Andromeda Galaxy

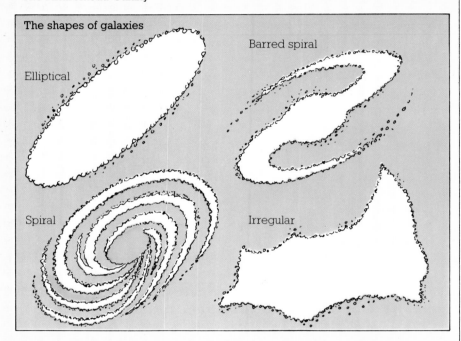

The shapes of galaxies

Elliptical

Barred spiral

Spiral

Irregular

Quasars

The most energetic of all known objects are the distant quasars. These are probably young galaxies still collapsing from huge gas clouds, which are dominated by a colossal black hole. Its gravity swirls infalling gases around at speeds close to that of light. These swirling gases generate energy and eject jets of matter.

A quasar – 3C 273

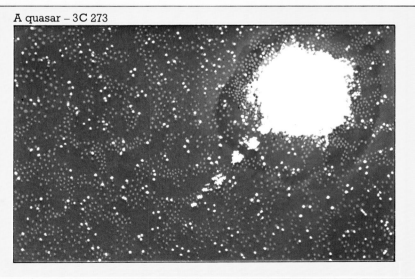

The Big Bang

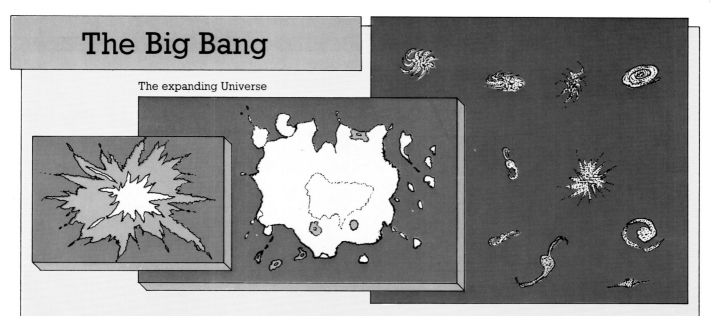

The expanding Universe

Every galaxy in the Universe is moving away from every other galaxy. The Universe is expanding and we can calculate that this expansion must have begun about 15 billion years ago. We cannot go back any further than this, because no events occurred to measure time by: time itself did not exist.

At the instant of the Big Bang – the start of the expansion – the Universe must have been unimaginably dense and hot. As it cooled and expanded, giant clouds of gas slowly clumped together under the pull of gravity Each cloud fragmented into stars, forming the first galaxies. Many of these –

like the quasars – suffered violent outbursts as the infall of gas slowly came to an end. Galaxies are still being carried away from one another by the expansion of the Universe, which may continue forever if there is too little matter in the Universe for gravity to pull it together again.

New Questions

Due for launch by the Space Shuttle in 1985, the Space Telescope has a 2.4 m (94 inch) mirror. It will be above the Earth's atmosphere and be able to see celestial objects a hundred times fainter than those which can be seen from Earth. Astronomers can only guess at some of the wonders which the Space Telescope will reveal. But they are certain that it will raise many new questions about the nature of the Universe.

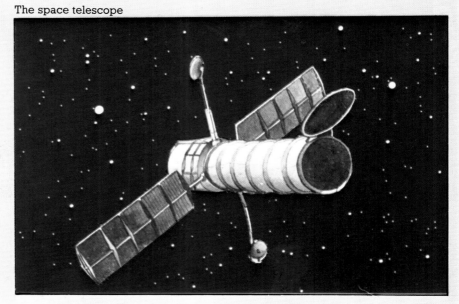

The space telescope

Glossary

Atom The smallest part of an element that can exist. Each element, such as hydrogen, helium, and carbon, for example, has its own unique atomic structure.

Billion A billion in this book is equal to one thousand million.

Black hole A body whose gravity is so strong that nothing – not even light – can escape its pull.

Centrifugal force An apparent force that pulls outward on any body moving in a curved path. It is the tendency of the body to move in a straight line and resist being made to follow a curve.

Constellation A recognizable pattern of stars in the sky. Constellations are only grouped together from our viewpoint, and the stars comprising them may be separated by great distances in space.

Electromagnetic radiation A stream of electrical and magnetic energy which travels through space at the speed of light. Bodies in space give out different types of electromagnetic radiation – light, X rays and gamma rays, for example – depending on the processes going on inside them.

Globular cluster A globe-shaped cluster of old, red stars found at the outer edges of a galaxy.

Gravity The force of attraction that acts between two objects. The more massive an object is, and the closer it is, the greater is its gravitational force.

Light year A measure of distance used by astronomers. It is the distance that light travels in a year – 9.46 thousand billion km (5.88 thousand billion miles).

Nebula A vast cloud of dust and gas in which stars are born. See also *Planetary nebula*.

Planetary nebula A shell of gas gently ejected from an old star nearing the end of its life. It looks a bit like the disk of a planet when seen through a telescope.

Quasar The central core of a young active galaxy. Quasars are the most distant and energetic objects in the Universe.

Red giant An old star whose core has collapsed and heated up, and whose outer layers have been forced to billow out and cool down. Some red giants are 300 times the size of the Sun.

Supergiant A late stage in the life of a massive star. Supergiants can be more than 1,000 times the size of the Sun and millions of times brighter.

Supernova The explosion of a massive star at the end of its life. For a brief period, a supernova shines billions of times brighter than an ordinary star.

White dwarf A dying star which has run out of fuel. Most stars reach this stage after a brief spell as a red giant.

Index

PRINTED IN BELGIUM BY

proost

INTERNATIONAL BOOK PRODUCTION